MW01284286

Also by the author

Apocalypse Rose, Auerhahn Press, 1967
Neon Poems, Atom Mind Publications, 1970
The Last of the Moccasins, City Lights Books, 1971
                                    Mother Road Publications, 1996
Over the Stage of Kansas, Telephone Books, 1973
The Trashing of America, Kulchur Foundation, 1975
Blue Orchid Numero Uno, Telephone Books, 1977
Are you a Kid?, Cherry Valley Editions, 1977
Moccasins Ein Beat-Kaleidoskop, Europaverlag, 1980
Panik in Dodge City, Expanded Media Editions, 1983
Forever Wider, 1954–1984, Scarecrow Press, 1985
Was Poe Afraid?, Bogg Publications, 1990
Journals from Lysidia, Synesthesia Press, 1999
Reefer Madness in the Age of Apostasy, Butcher Shop Press, 2000
Hand on the Doorknob, Water Row Books, 2000
Cut Here, 12 Gauge Press, 2002
In Memory of My Father, Cherry Valley Editions, 2003
Some Mothers' Sons, Cherry Valley Editions, 2004
Choix de poèmes, Wigwam, 2007
Eat Not Thy Mind, Glass Eye Books/Ecstatic Peace Library, 2010
Animal Light, Verlag Peter Engstler, 2012
Tent Shaker Vortex Voice, Bottle of Smoke Press, 2012
Benzedrine Highway, Kicks Books, 2013
Planet Chernobyl, Verlag Peter Engstler, 2015
Apocalypse Rose, Lenka Lente, 2015
Incognito, Ergo Sum, Ragged Lion Press, 2016
Camposque Verentis, Cherry Valley Editions, 2017
Cowboy of the Ancient Sea, Bottle of Smoke Press, 2018
Le Dernier des Moccasins, Sonatine, 2021
Of Myth & Men, Bottle of Smoke Press, 2021

Tent Shaker Vortex Voice

Tent Shaker Vortex Voice

Charles Plymell

Bottle of Smoke Press

2022

ISBN-13   978-1-937073-35-0 (Paperback)

First Printing, October 2012
Second Printing, April 2013
Third Printing, September 2013
Fourth Printing, October, 2022

Bottle of Smoke Press
8 Bridle Way
Wappingers Falls, NY 12590

orders@bospress.net
www.bospress.net

PROLEGOMENON

The complexity of form, fact, and prophecy in this Tent Shaker Vortex Voice warrants a discussion of its creation and influence. I have drawn upon Lucretius and Loren Eiseley. I am reminded of George Steiner's observation that all poetry is a 400 (plus) year look backward to the words of Shakespeare. Not altogether; the bard himself, with many great thinkers from Darwin to modern atomic theorists looked back to (if not borrowed from) Lucretius, who wrote 21 (plus) centuries ago. Shakespeare indeed may have versified his amalgamated chemistries of connotative & denotative meanings in his sonnets and plays to foil his critics, while Lucretius may have lain latent from his critics because of faulty flowery translations by poets through the centuries. Stylistically, his great poem is more like prose with heightened poetic flourishes. I thought too that Eiseley's poetry was more in his prose and one time suggested that his prose was superior poetry to his verse. He of course, replied to my foolish observation, humbly recalling how hard it is for him to place his words.

I have been influenced by Lucretius and his history of Nature. He offered an alternative to the pain and suffering concomitant to abstract beliefs in gods needed for the human psyche. Today, the need has increased along with the pain, suffering and death that has grown exponentially with population in method, madness, sickness, and machinery that religions have brought since the pre-Christian days of Lucretius. Invention itself, has fed the kill. Coincidentally, it was Loren Eiseley who posited that humans & dolphins are equal in intelligence but the hand itself propagated mankind's machinations.

Loren Eiseley and I both spent our youth above the ancient sea. I first read him in the 1950's. I was born in 1935 in a dust storm south of his Platte River country not far from the Chalk Pyramids in northern Kansas. I hypothesized that a body from outer space exploded and left the geographical "Big Sink" south of the pyramids. As a child living in Kansas, I had "space dreams" of geometrical forms "chaos theory" crossing in planes and lines and more vivid fractal dimensions as I awoke in fright. There were certainly travelers who crossed paths there, and alien creatures from the deep that can be seen by following links on the Kansas Chalk Pyramids. Sharks teeth can be found there as well as rare skeletal remains in museums of the area. In the same county, Gove County, "Kansas Pop Rocks" or "Boji stones" can be found. Now they are used in New Age healing to align Chakra points of energy in the body. The rocks are both male and female and one can feel energy in them. The females are always smooth egg shaped, yet a bit flatter. The male rocks always have geometrical forms suggesting sacred geometry like that of Descartes. The male can also be peppered with the prime number 1 of the ancient Mari system. There are occasional hermaphrodites that have both characteristics. A force can be felt within the rocks. I have made sculpture pieces to hold mine as they have an affinity to iron. I think it was Lao Tze who said rocks are hot on the inside and cold on the outside.

Early tribes crossed at the point in the pyramids called the "Eye of the Needle." That point was the intersection where Hopi traveled in the four directions connecting with the Mayans far to the south. It was the farthest north for the Navajo and used throughout history as a landmark where tribes and herds convened. I happened there with my son when I was going to do a book on Kansas for a subsidiary of Random House. We visited almost every historical spot in Kansas and ended up under the "Eye of the Needle." It was there, miles from anyone or anything, that we heard the "Voice." It sent shivers up our backs as we looked at each other in awe. It was a voice of neither man nor beast, more an echo from deep space, the primal universe, the quaking of heavens. I didn't feel like finishing the book and put it aside. I thought about the Voice for years and its prophetic amplification was always in the back of my mind. By chance, I learned what the voice was when reading Loren Eiseley's essay "The Dance of Frogs" in his book, The Star Thrower. The explanation from the medium's cabinet was made clear by old "Dreyer's low, troubled voice..." He had heard the "Voice" too. For me the Voice became a prophecy to fill as the Eye of the Needle crumbled. I looked around to see that the apocalypse wasn't the future but was happening now in increments all around us. The "Game Lord" had spoken. We hadn't made our altruistic place in the eyes of the innocents, but rather used our eyes and hands to destroy our innocence.

As a mythographer, an historian of the unconscious, a Kansa shaman, I've also been influenced by surrealist images like Hart Crane's: "A serpent swam a vertex to the sun / on unpaced beaches leaned its tongue and drummed" and Pound's energy and parabolic form of the Cantos. Other poets and artists like Bob Branaman who came out of the "vortex" mythologized it as a place that pulled one back at times returning to this energy and its center. This artistic observation indeed piqued the curiosity of the poet, Allen Ginsberg, who came to Wichita to experience the vortex and wrote a long poem celebrating his pilgrimage. He was aware, of course, of the literary Vorticist movement. The preceding generations who migrated to San Francisco bringing the Wichita influence had experienced the literary canons in their academic studies as well. I was in a later wave and my interpretation of the vortex became more cosmic. At that time I was a high school dropout not having a formal education but had read Pound, Hart Crane and Shakespeare as part of my subculture hipster lifestyle of the street.

Rt. 66 was not my epiphany of the open road, but rather my commute from K.C. to L.A. begun in the 30's and continued beyond the 60's. When not on the road, I spent my youth riding over, yes, plowing or riding high in a combine thrashing wheat or driving a truck over that ancient sea with not a soul in sight, shouting into the void around me; seeing a speck on the horizon become a windmill, a barn, a lone cottonwood, a frontal mirage, moving with me, never reaching the eternal edge of its blue sky.

PROLOGUE

Under the Kansa plains was a sea of aphotic antiquity where lived pre-historic creatures; fiendish, silent & sanguinary beyond any film-maker's special effects millions of years hence that scare children in electronic game & transformer images of reality.

In haunting silence, entire universes of seas and skies radiated in dark matter above the horror of drowned time, wrapped their vortices and stirring shrouds of freeze-dried star blood in distant space that forever displayed moon & earth & other planet beads along the strings of space.

Oxygen & water set the stage for sub-atomic bacchanal chemistries of every form where life grew under scattered cotton clouds & played in eons of deep time from cannibal liquid neon-gnaw aglow of Black Dragon fish darting through gruesome cavernous shadows to underworld sharks flashing millions of years in sleek engine of survival evolution captured by human hands' aquariums; their dead teeth found dry today in Kansa Chalk Pyramids perfecting growth art and form by time, wind, and water's hypnotic autumns, the smells of mountain's smoky air bringing life's mad swoon to the corners of the sky as voices cry aloud in the blind elements at the gate of all deaths slinking terrors of slow change in eternal mind-splayed force itself, luring ghosts of all living matter when battles of the pitiful slain chew guilty frontal brains in time's feed lots all around us, but you don't see them now.

It is here, the Mysterious Rocks are scattered in dust & dew like gametic dancing space roots void of matter or magnetic motion, the female rock smooth, the male battle marks decoding messages from millenary ghosts entangled, barbed in the land, time and wilderness ridden over by demon men with twisted DNA like legs of coyotes hung on fence post to flee cowardly time until the wolf will run like the shape of the U.S. mapping mankind's striking force-shredded flesh that civilization found scattered across its karmas and coincidences & Siris galore in random carnival capes of Mother Earth's travail of ripped flesh revenge. A great needle threaded by cyclonic vision so vast it pierced the void before the eyes of living creatures in a voice long & low pulled their heartbeats around the séance of atom bells where orphan lives lost again threw off their cauls in the upheaval She reclaims.

WE HEARD THE GAME LORD SPEAK
ITS TONGUE BECAME THE VISION

(Animals learn from Nature.
Man must learn from Animals
to understand Nature's reprisal.)

Voice out of Kansa sky rolled out upon the prairie in
        quanta sound waves ceremony joined of wolf howl
           intense above the Chalk Pyramids around a
mirage of skulls and bones migrating to the horizons
        into outlines of creatures killed in highway death
cyclone nature years of history shredded in tornado vision
        of dead Buffalo eyes in the vortex hollow world globes
        of home to creatures who lived beyond our scan.

Nature's blind terror tempest prepares her thunderbolts.

All suffered forevermore man animal voice of space void
        of hands and brains to conquer, attack, render
destruction in the name power taught in all curricula
        to become aware of death in first written history
or discuss afterlife of the abstract gods
        while elephants sensed their burial place.

        When man fashioned his death with hands
        instead of fins of innocent dolphin play
hands from toxin depth clapping at Special Olympics
        brings party coils to the last amputated mind
with ribbons on chest, medals long forgotten
        victories won in great sports arenas of abstract gods
afterlife never thought of in cheers & peanuts & bubble gum
        all explode now and warriors with their limbs cut off
        visions without answers unaware of why the battle
existential bow upon its violin of pain from old camps
        heroic, ironic fate; the creator, destroyer, preserver.

The collateral Cross in a world of pain and suffering
        scalps floated like paper folders from the world of trade
        a prelude to insanity when Nature reclaims its domain
in ancient games of power death's rewards in bright lights
        make the earth shake with fire and water and wind
killing all with one swath not choosing good or evil
        storms come more frequent, destruction all around
family spared they say by their god and faith
        but the child lands in field two miles away
her mother and father lay dead ruins once town
        redress of fire and wind in the Game Lord's voice
savaged by man once in Nature's hands
the Lord must have his hand on our shoulder
        one man says, his house spared from scorched earth
his neighbors houses in ashes all around.

At Gettysburg they carried their cut-off limbs
        and today industry of war defends liberty they say
        in our longest war power and wealth from spent kill
enslaved again by wealth of artificial limbs, the pharmaceuticals
gunpowder, tanks, grenades, & rifles spread around the world
        from oil power to run the smooth lies safe in history
        the child will not learn the lesson in schools when the new
merchants of death can't say what we are fighting for
        slaughter of men and innocent creatures loyal animals
the long snake tortured and hacked in pieces
        squirms back and bite itself in severed sting
        the animal chews its leg from the trap
in battle the penis is cut off and stuffed in the dead mouth
        the blade, the steel, knives, poison chemicals in a box
           blown up bits of flesh are found in bagels and lox
            ization flourishes alongside suffering.

           g leaves awakened the spirit once again
           Lord hypnotic temples tallies guilty pleas
           pped tumbleweed set free in erratic winds

the clouds are in no hurry the same tale to tell
      the signals of branded stars spark in still position
      zigzagging protons travel in sun and space
      their journey as long as the lifetime of the universe
      other journeys of sperm and newborns awake
within their canyons open tombs quake
      ocean's giant hand grabs from the deep
      indiscriminate of what it takes from lands far away
      where the last whale is tangled in man's net
of politicians, pimps & kings authority of avarice
      learn lives are not discriminatory in Nature's purge
where humans failed & brought wrath on population surge.

People entangled in their lands pray and fold their hands
      scattered into empty matter frail and pitiful
blind elements shut them in trapped terrors of the mind
      wilderness at the gates of death they dispel
seized by words the last generation died of hell.

Apache greeted a Moor and three Spanish warriors
      first men to cross Atlantis seen in lower river valley
the native stretched out his arms and opened hand
his palms turned upward to the Sun's burning voice
      born into the universe & the ancient sea a new land.

Followed Coronado toward the pyramids &
      the mysterious rocks & sunken sea where the gold turned
black and liquid 500 years later in time land curse greed
      that grinds into every how-to chessboard war game
while Charles V conquers Tunis & frees 20,000 Christian slaves
      killed the philosopher Pagans and triumphal
      born again message whorls to great velocity in
      new toxic islands washing ashore
in sacrificial blood on the altar of science.
In Arizona, Apache slaves fought back until
      the air condition population devoured them too

Gila monster in a shadow traced by the airplane
   people sold their trinkets for a boomerang tattoo.

Shark teeth and crafted arrow from ancient sea
   Navajo trail north with gentle breeze
   Hopi crossed the eye of needle South to Aztec land
then East they went to Potawatami sand
   Sioux came West all gathered at one point
   the double spiral and parabola to anoint.

Radiant time dancing in the dark matter of eons
   a prairie rider sat on his horse
watching a calf kick up its legs
   "Everything wants to live."

Feral eyes avoided humans at their peril
   and the calf will be taken as its mother
smells the warm hay where it lay
   until the great steel blades of matter
cuts out its hunger for the fatter.

The President told Black Kettle to wave the flag
   when riders thundered across the sage
   but the tornado comes to take all
   no matter identity, name on mailbox, or age.

The children knew to lie flat in the gullies
   of rattlers giving warning to soft moccasins
unlike poison of a God-fearing minister and
   devil forked tongue of riders for religion.

The sky becomes a snake of galaxies eating its tail
   minister's men cut out the squaw's private parts
   to decorate their saddle horns
cut off their breasts to make purses of
   to sell as souvenirs in Tenderloin, San Francisco.

Babe in the arm of butchered mothers
        screaming on the prairie fell to the sod.
        The riders ground them into loaves
        of bloody dirt under the horse's hooves.

        Streets full of flags one unexpected day
rubble and blood many times over
        cleans its spirit the great winds say.

Step up to the plate and play ball, pray and hope your
        house will not be washed away like
        civilizations that carry flags of conquered lands.

The Moor wore black flag around his head
        feathers and hats would adorn those who
        covered their footprints in revenge of dust
        fought back when taken slaves in new world
        filled the ancient sea dead chemistry, geology, and industry
        bones piled on flint and arrows while
Michelangelo put finishing touches on his last judgment
        of Nature's hand reclaiming itself
        voices in the new world shouting hallelujah .

In Arizona the same policy forever to sell guns
        and defraud the government of goods
to starve Indians in their designated places
        give outdated weapons until they have to raid
        for their necessary food
cut them down with superior weaponry
        arms for money, same policy forever
shades of the Arab Spring
        manifest destiny in smuggled drugs
        fossilized shadows stand by bodies of cactus.

Immigrants built the skyscrapers
        walked high to decide the world

balanced on beams daring as a circus act
        wore Fedoras not hard hats, tossed hot rivets
overpopulation waits for earth to blow up or turn
        spreading cancerous anthills in piles of waste
        when nature regurgitates in quakes and shakes
and the children have nothing to learn.

Its great hand reaches up from the ocean floor
        islands of waste floating towards the wind
tornadoes find new alleys of devastation
        ships overturn and slide into cosmic caves
        sun flares traveling at the speed of life never end
a spirit locked in elliptic phase of the ocean wave
        ride in gallows above the frenzy of the sea.

Each morning the savage beast is born again
        a faint resemblance wilts in the ozone layer
magic among brothers of Nez Perce Sioux and the Crow
        painted eyes like a raccoon
        the photograph would steal his spirit to show.

Wealth of those gone feral on 5th Ave.
        left the homeless sleeping on a grate to keep warm
gifts of the elements that wild animals sense
        beg until the hand freezes the fingerprint.

Dolphins made no coins nor created empires
have no abstractions derived from greed and fame
where beauty survives for the human eye
        from promoters of popularity for art's sake
in suburban sameness of soul-less shooters
        religious traps or wrapped tar-paper shacks
it's all make believe in hype and eye.

They no longer ride the horse without a saddle
        or walk steel beams high above the streets
        revolution comes and goes like a revolving door

Jack Palance to Burt Lancaster "Revolution is a whore"
        the Professionals sleep now, too
they shoot horses don't they
        out beyond the silver curtained night.

Flags fly high over the sea creatures, snakes,
        animal and human bones buried in sod
compost of blood & terror within the blaze
        Angelfish fusing female skin to its side
Siamese forever in circle of one not alone
        the dust on window shades sunlight brings
Pre-history to Kansa land of winds
        flags whipping in the smell ozone
above the rattler who knows the ground is shaking
        when the buffalo has black holes for eyes
and indiscriminate wrath opens the horizon.

The chalk pyramids crumble like civilizations on
        human paths following the herds around
        buoy & burden vessel of long-dried sea who
sat by the rocks and made signs from voices
        ideas of right and wrong and
        rattles cut off by same shovel
that plant the seed in the earth of life
        where animals die and roll silent as quilts.

A fear of death makes humans kill
        the seed of chance carries in time
        procreating the blood of sun waiting to
drench particles in eons forming flags and steel.

North, South, East and West the wind talked
        to Game Lord in Tent Shaker's Voice.

For every form of life a cloud could make
an angry cyclone can indiscriminately take.

Light comes through the rocks in New Mexico
        things too great to conceive
leave a trace, a feeling, a path of
        paradigms for other wonders from the void
man in armored vehicles crawling through explosions
        slap another merchant on back.

(The moon shines in night's full light
the earth is aroused as when a woman bathes
turns in her phases bringing blood to half the earth
of men's rallied avarice and ambition and battle cry
of eternal wars we do not know women would wage
the eternal wound I know not of but almost certain
that the eternal sores of life are fed by fear of death
and my remorse is forever lasting as empty space
knowing that battles and wars will continue when
earth falls ill with battle and thunderous wars from
every side to keep the blood of innocence flowing
collaterally damaged fatally wounded virgin birth.
When eyeless nights rob you from the year
and jewels of nature are no longer found
but scraps of tin from ancient roadside tinker men
now buried alongside the tossed Budweiser can
and shards of bottles glint for moonlight's
distant bulb from kitchen light alone on prairie sod
like lantern flicker in the corner of the night.
Rusty diner neon signs gone waitress love grime
an apron in roadside rubble cactus blossom rots
lost kiss against the numb thruway battered cheek
the gas attendant gone, the sunflowers tip their
heads to sundown and pack night mysteries
of the universe tight in flirt of coffee cup drips.
Void and matter beckon on the party line of truth

words stuck to viper's tongues ready to strike
banned from new vocabularies of the smart phone.
The Denver sandwich now the Western Omelet
menus of numb consciousness of truck driver's
whore walking in human form of ghostly rhythms
of the earth leaking like contents of a broken jar
one thing no longer illuminates another dead end
you leave once more....
　　　　　car readied to the Northwest winds.)
The smell of incense voices of those who listened
　　　　to "The Argument" have joined new age
　　　　body spirits torn in the winds of eternity
dissipated into the commerce of the day.
　　　　Those who once climbed your ladder
bow their heads like the broken rungs
　　　　we've known so well where talent failed
to signal their sycophants to be silent
　　　　creativity but a word, not a life.
The visit over in the wake of climb without ascent
　　　　that graced memory's spirits they've never known
lesser arguments piled draught in compost bones.

Where the beggared are buggered I look
from my window bald men in strontium wind
communicate into their hand-held devices mouth to ear
space annihilated once traveled by riders with messages
or couriers of doorbells not rung under liquid cola signs
hold the words and colors forever in neon diner sign
of silent death settling in leukemia evenings of suffering
where Christians drag their pains to Easter worship in
discourse of the hand's reflective argument of humans
persist in first beginning that created intelligent design
as if empiricism could rise again to answer the simple
observation of reflected afternoon sunlit prism spots
going crazy on my walls but not reflecting in my mirror.
Germs from the Old World chemical air over Brooklyn Bridge

Mob loan-sharking dates back to Rome Little Caesar himself
charged 100% thousands of years before James Cagney,
Little Italy or the Federal Reserve on a larger scale collapse
powerful derivatives more than usury no real assets left
can't help but rob the poor to give to the rich once more
In the world's largest pyramid scheme in derivative arts
put Viagra in water and have populist hard-on for hours.
Christ will always forgive the evangelist in tears
or the confessor's armaments of altruism at the Cross
ratified in the genes of Crown and the Conquerors
Captain Marvel's holy moley hero megalopolis Batman
Ho-hum of Buddha watching TV in mortgaged home
Armageddon fairy tale with special effects men on knees
with ass to nose more easily understood than virgin birth
civilization's language lost to the T-shirt amazing logos.
Goering's attack: denounce the pacifists; democracy,
parliament, dictatorship it works the same in every country.
The Olympians of good health, good homes, good vitamins
would make him proud, but a gene pool is always for itself).

America ... the wasted buffalo killed for sport
            each with a universes in their globed eyes
            as has every innocent creature
who will forever watch the half politician reload.
Communism and Capitalism in war all the time
            other countries warring around their edges
Capitalism and Communism both the same
            killing the young to feed them while both failed.

Can't get the kids to learn
            Nature has no use for words
            uttered from death row minds
            no one has broken out of death tomb
            their arts and culture & boutique grinds.
Those who know nothing bow to everything
            caught doing time of new rules new game
            the convict knows ignorance and authority

bum's barrel fires, butt in one hand, bottle in the other
        lying on the street or huddled unkempt, unregulated
regretful for something they did or said along the way
        fucked over by the opportunist with a new cause
a right-minded person, over there, to be sure, a square
sickness, death, O.D., the cure, always something
        and always radiation silently inserting itself.
(My sister found dead near Indian bar on Valencia Street, S.F.)
never knew what they were fighting about in drunken stupor
lost tribes burned in that Chinese lantern of the Western Moon
I see the shipwreck & spacesuit high above the sunflower.
There might be a hologram at the edge of space indeed to hold
old captains afraid to sail beyond the seas tangled in the ropes.

I have only chance to pray to and long for the bodies in my bed
Displayed in desperation on the screen flickering cooperation
That have claimed like figurines my possibilities & weary dream
Nothingness has ever been more profound to the boy on a bike
Pedaling into unknown possibilities all over and again each day
Oblivious to the eternal connection of love beyond the playmate
Carrying in him the basic traits of human politics and a history
Of cheating, lying, stealing all tattooed once more in the years
To come clinging like lichen to the seawreck'd hope of shore
If only displayed in artificial form as parasite, vamp, old whore
I've climbed that rigging and never fell but to the hype & prize
I've held on to the wheel alongside the road of progress like
The grass, the weeds always half beaten down & sorrowful
Dandelion pride under the feet of those who walk unaware
alone in piano snow; the keys busted caught me digging
hitch a ride from the grey area, take a bend in the road going
South out of South Bend somewhere to the Delta cotton dirt
pure polka dot shirt flies in the wind from medium's cabinet.

Einstein, our modern oracle
spoke in equations rhetorical.
Since him, the nuclear claw
dredged life from sacred maw.

Changes your mind when darkness comes
and time to die makes a raging coward lie

Faces on her dollar bills forever left
A bellowing entry fee for life lost care
Curricula vita of linens and underwear

Is there a spirit you made of your son to sacrifice for me
over the billions of light years that made life on earth?
If so it was good and what to do but whimper and confess
I failed to see, I failed to live, now I can't fail to die.
I am not the Brave riding bareback over tomahawk hill
and now the mystery of a world on the other side
where everyone good joins together again like in a movie
with a happy ending of who is dancing in forgotten dust.

POSTSCRIPT

PLANET CHERNOBYL

Hiroshima Nagasaki, Fukushima and Chernobyl
The silent death radiates in suburban ennui
They call me Dr. Faustus of the abandoned universe
of a never-ending chain of paper dolls.
The buzzing fly's string path invisible under the reactors.
I trade with the devil and buy used souls and your best minds
Hiroshima, Nagasaki, Fukushima and Chernobyl today
tomorrow the Mississippi, Hudson and San Andreas
the last gasp of all the living creatures on dying planet
blind radioactive paradise to China and the dead Dead Sea
You'll never see me the sub-atomic particles of time
open the great fissure to find out who abandoned them
down to where the sea claws gather them in poisoned pods.
The best minds of a generation split the atom that
Whitman sang belongs to each, now breathe the air and
split the cells that spiral to their own instructions to duplicate.
Radioactive cancer of times found the best minds in New Mexico
power from agencies overhanging Apache dark eyes no more.
Energy lines & high wires modern icons on the landscape
Scientists smash particles like angry kids at play and the devil
knows the price of soul and in white lab-coats throw Frisbees,
and know a thing or two about equations to build
the abandoned planet of catastrophe in zone of no choice
nothing but hands and in the sea are dolphins with brains.
Flee the soldier, liquidators and the criminal minds
when karma of coyote piss is bottled for perfume and
vodka is made of bleach & kerosene to keep the
hair & skin from sticking to the pillows at night
darkness comes over the game of win against whom
the atom or the physics or the universe of nothing.

A self-replicating medal to pin upon them while the
trees are scared too but they are quiet as a meltdown
the ancient Scorpion bombs genetic jails full of fear
until prison consciousness collides with larger culture
civilizations of souls smash in particle accelerator
Virtual mutant gene pools rising like tsunami
giant hand around planet breaks from its beads.

Tear down Kentucky mountains and fill the seas
with garbage real basic real fast fate of species
creating ourselves into techno-robots with our hands
no fear of death, comes with price no war, no soul.
Tracks of unknown Acuras and Cadillac gasoline
spent radon forever in petrified creature museums
back to die of shock when daylight breaks the hourglass
drums dream of nuclear fires on wretched soil
already mystery of different people's disease
who know how to live in terror as a natural habitat
planet plugged with scraps of clothing, bones,
concrete, books, newspapers, stolen skates, dying birds
and the streets change without notice into
black sky nuke neon drugstore of new cures.

Human in the shadows of good and evil hydra hearts
and hands that built the world of energy from splitting
invisible secrets that pushed buttons for generations
into dead zone looking for something familiar
to hear someone say we'll win ask the voices from
Chernobyl with radioactive foam on their lips and
Vodka eyes listening to the beeps and silent clicks
biggest killer of all galvanizes skin radiation rising
Hiroshima, Nagasaki, Fukushima, and Chernobyl
where neurotoxins in the wind fades old glory gold
seagulls in the sky beneath the blood moon time
and space blinded self-replication Mississippi too.
Chernobyl with the hunted dosimeter and guns of

liquidators and animals crying looking in the eyes
of humans who control their fate again and again
one government with the gun of nuclear power and
military secrets national energy secrets arm sales
in a pact and prayer of old incantations of nowhere.

Gazing into eternities of toxic sunsets wiped clear
sulphur settles in place where skin sheds the leper
on the lizard's last rock hot on the inside and
cold on the out where it all began to lay waste
in the name of power and physics new childhood maladies
while last punk band plays on to one million raised hands
COATTAIL JESUS AND HIS HOUNDS OF HEAVEN.

In every eye the universe in every creature the eye
the machine entangles animal life and time as loud as the
blasts that blows flesh in the bagels of outdoor coffee shops
black skies not far away fire falls beyond the razor-edge fences
of those who go to bed alone like the fish in the sea finally
of all the blood of reality into compost of radioactivity
mountains of poison topped to bury earth in the earth
and stream under the pulsar stars at the edge of time
coal fire bigger than the mountains of eternity in the event
of the unknowable psyche they all came to see the dolls
wearing the bling perpetual self forever exploited by love
in the econoline van that brings body & soul of love
erupting in a plume delivered in right time and space
address of the bird's song unheard by human occupancy
Sappho's distant cry when her bird died is heard still
the island child continuing its toil and hunger for life
Egyptian blood spills into sand of thousands of years
Geiger chatter replacing chants & songs of revolutions
carbon & crystal separate at undecipherable boundaries of the
dream alone in flight fascinated and frightened like shy animus
that escaped the sale to the devil
living for hundreds of thousands of years

under the sarcophagus or silent waters of the Hudson
we breath silent clicks of radioactive dust or PCBs
the urge to purge and puke through trash of cancer cells
and last change of clothing where senators of gluttony
graze like livestock to rape the sage they sat next to in school
and gnarl and rasp and grate and scratch rotten skin
doomed like innocent creatures in feed lots of television's
empty insane trunk where drunken computer chips
explode into cosmic dust forever detected cells
in blood of hard mud pies lung and liver pouring
from the mouths of blind throne empires lost lamps
shining like moonlight over the radiant seal's back.

Mr. Nuke, Dr. Devil, Mephistopheles, Christ O Mighty,
Messier Split of radioactive coffins in Isotope Russia
Japan and half-life America the material toxin pile.
Beyond the Federal Zone and nuclear wash
hanging forever clotheslines of plutonium
lace panties from eternity's wash, doll's eyes
consciousness captured in a crystal lattice
all animals dying from lack of love and care.
They are hungry and sick with radiation
liquidators shoot them like collateral bodies
under the breath of silent clicks of radioactive dust
that formed the brains of battlefields forever war
under merciful God who will comfort devil's wealth
can hold out to the last person but try to escape
like the poached elephant dead, only predator man,
its baby won't leave but dies of love trauma unseen
in Africa unheard as the prayers to escape nature
beyond Japan, beyond San Andreas, the Hudson,
the great Missouri rolls on like the lesson of Russia
Wars were nothing and now the real terror begins
in racial senescence of each breath & memory of the
apocalypse arriving in increments, look around you.

FINI

Charles Plymell, Outlaw Poet, born in 1935 Kansas dust storm.

Colophon

Tent Shaker Vortex Voice was designed and typeset by Bill Roberts in New York. The text was set in Brioso Pro and Krete

Made in the USA
Columbia, SC
30 October 2024

45306898R00022